AWAKENING

GERRY MILLER

for Max – a memento

Published by Oswica

All rights reserved

© Gerry Miller 2004

ISBN 0-9548251-0-1

Printed in Northern Ireland by
Universities Press Ltd

The private thoughts of a private person. This collection of poetry and pictures is a reflection upon scenes of love and violence, inhumanity and hope, recollections and aspirations – all of which contribute to the composition of life, and with which we can identify in a personal way.

Thanks

to Michelle and Leanne and their families, who are my greatest inspiration and support, in good times and bad;

to my wider family circle and dear friends, who make life worth living;

to Gavin, Orsi and Emily, who helped put life in perspective;

to Kerry and Keith, who pushed me in the right direction;

and to you, the reader, with whom I am privileged to share my deepest thoughts and emotions.

Enjoy!

CONTENTS

A REMINDER	7
THERE IS A TIME	9
THE VISIT	11
LOVE	13
COMBER, Northern Ireland	14
DONAGHADEE, Northern Ireland	17
HOLYWOOD, Northern Ireland	19
NEWTOWNARDS, Northern Ireland	21
SHAFTS OF DARKNESS	23
AWAKENING	25
METAMORPHOSIS	26
THE ACCOUNT	28
THE MUSIC OF LIFE, Bergen, Norway	31
SYKKYLVEN, Norway	33
LOOK BRAVELY TO THE FUTURE	34
A TIME OF TRUTH	36
THE CHURCH AT ÅSANE, Norway	39
FROM A MIDNIGHT SUN	41
TOMORROW	43
CASCADE OF MEMORIES	45
INCUBUS	47
THE BISHOP'S INVITATION	49
BUDAPEST, Hungary	51
TRAVELLING NORTH	53
WHEN TIME HEALS	55
TROUBLED TIMES	57
SELJA AND SUNNIVA, Norway	59
LIVING THE DAY	61
THE CYCLE	63
NOTES	64

A Reminder of Humility

TO MY ENGLISH TEACHER

Can you analyse every poem, dear English Teacher?
If Keats, Wordsworth or Hopkins stood
At the front of the classroom and rapped your knuckles
Each time you interpreted their thoughts wrongly,
Would your knuckles not be very sore?
You have an answer for every line.
Some I agree with, others not.
And yet others I think only the poet himself
Will ever understand.
There are poems like this.

Dear English Teacher,
I know you could not crack
The combination of my mind always.

Gavin Weston, 1979.

Giant's Causeway, Northern Ireland

THERE IS A TIME

There is a time which some call dusk,
when things we knew begin to fade
and lose the spark which once they had.

There is a time which some call dark,
when things we knew just disappear
and leave a void which once they filled.

There is a time which some call dawn,
when things unclear begin to form
and take a shape unknown before.

There is a time which some call day,
when all is bright and clear and new.

That is the time which some call love.
And it is good.
And it is now.

THE VISIT

When I was at my first school
I used to pass my grandmother's house on the way home.
Every day I called to see her
and had a biscuit and a glass of milk.

She would always ask about my day at school
and loved to hear me recite a poem
or read a passage from our reading book.

Sometimes there would be long silences
and then I was glad to get away
and used to run up the road to our house.

On my eighth birthday
she was asleep in her chair beside the fire.
On the table was my milk and a present wrapped in paper.

I drank the milk quietly,
took the present,
and closed the door gently as I went out.

When I got home and told my mother
she put her coat on and ran down the road
as fast as her legs would carry her.

I will never know whether I should have kissed her
or tried to waken her.
I will always remember how happy she looked.

'Fusion of Feelings', County Down

LOVE

Love is a meeting of minds;
a fusion of feelings;
a coupling of chemistry.

Walks by the waterside;
wandering through woods;
whispering in wilderness
of wishes and wants.

Memories of meetings;
weekends of wistfulness;
raptures of romance;
agonies of angst.

Hopes that bring happiness
larger than living:
more real than reality;
more lasting than life.

COMBER, County Down

Our favourite walk is up the Glen Road.
White hawthorn, rosehips and blackberry
are all there at their time for the discerning eye;
and the road meanders for three miles away from the village
through the country and towards the big smoke of Belfast.
At the little bridge across the river
today's traffic finds the turning hard,
but it must have been a welcome watering spot
for yesterday's engines of real horse power.

When we have rested there and then retrace our steps,
there is a wonderful point just where the road starts to drop.
From there we can see the old mill - a century of life -
with its tall chimney and cluster of mill houses
still wrapped in wreaths of chimney smoke and just as authentic
as any village scene depicted in the Folk Museum.
If we want to shatter the illusion we might discover
that much of the mill is sub-divided into hi-tec units
and many of the houses are gutted and re-designed.   If we want to.

Further round is the inevitable urban sprawl
with new houses sprouting overnight in people's gardens -
the way mushrooms used to do in those very fields.
I sympathise with the hapless citizens whose retirement dreams
have been shattered by diggers and J.C.B's where only cows had grazed.
There may be some smug sense of consolation in the fact
that the new arrivals will never earn the accolade of true townsfolk
and that the redbrick monsters will never erase my vivid memory
of majestic chestnut trees stripped of their fruit by generations.

On the other side of the town the tide conceals and reveals
a path out to the island and on a clear summer's day
this is a vantage point in technicolour
from which cascades a host of islands, yachts and beaded waves.
On misty days we turn the corners to meet the Viking longboats
as they disgorge the marauding invaders who left the splendid ruins
as a legacy to primeval virtue and integrity.
An ornithological paradise,
where birds seek refuge from Arctic dayless seas.

Island Hill, Comber, County Down

Donaghadee Harbour, County Down

DONAGHADEE, County Down

The 'Dee is my Ireland in miniature
with the mixture of old and new buildings
between the backcloth of hillocks and downs
and the ever-present foreground of natural elements -
in uneasy marriage from Orlock to The Commons
of land and sea - with man's endeavour to harness them both for himself.

The town is contoured within the grasp of man's creations – the historical
fort whose legends have awakened early interests in local history
as they are passed down by word of mouth from father to son;
and the self-contained unit of the harbour,
an endless source of activity and colour,
an artist's palette in a state of constant dimensional movement.

The seasons of nature make it four towns, not one.
Best seen when September's glory blends them all
as visitors and residents stretch the summer's pleasures,
as trees and foliage are flushed with colours and smells of autumn,
as tranquil seas are interspersed with wrack and spume.

A place for health-restoring trips in childhood
and nostalgic visits as the years wear on.
The sea-wind always there, but biting more in winter,
a sharp reminder of advancing time.
The lighthouse ever-watchful -
man's vain attempt to claim a mastery
over God's creation.

Johnny the Jig, Holywood, County Down

HOLYWOOD, County Down

Sanctus Boscus, Old Priory, and Johnny the Jig
roll off the tongue like a litany of praise,
and conjure up the convoluted history of Holywood
from holy place through ancient settlement to golden years.

Restricted in extension by the lough and hills
divided by the iron road and then the bypass,
the intermediary link that would not die,
amoeba-like took shape and form in elongated mass.

The magic conjured up by names like Plas Merdyn,
the meandering roads - Demense, Croft, Church and Whinney Hill -
like Medusa's fascinating locks
come snaking from the crown and tumble to the shoulders of the lough.

The vista from the Whinney Hill above the Folk Museum
preserves the integrity of the Holy Wood -
a fitting situation for the history of folk-lore and legends.
The Lord Mayor's residence and the Bishop's home,
reached by coloured streamers from the historic May-pole,
at the centre of love and laughter - and sorrow.

A twinkling ribbon along the foreshore of life,
a vital artery to the heart of the city,
a legend of its own, on its own, for its own.
The Holywood of yesterday, today, and to the end of time.

Scrabo Hill, Newtownards, County Down

NEWTOWNARDS, County Down

It's very much a lived-in place
this market town of Ards,
a junction first of ancient paths
for travellers and bards.

Early settlers on Scrabo Hill
left relics of their lives
in stone and bronze and copper through
which history survives.

Finian's monastery was built
where grew a holy tree,
some seven centuries before
Columba's holy see.

The Market Cross is evidence
of mediaeval fame;
and Scrabo Tower a later sign
of personal acclaim.

The last one hundred years have seen
various thoughts on war -
embodied in The Cenotaph
and statue in The Square.

This treasure chest is our very own
cultural legacy.
And what might be the next remains –
For our posterity?

In 1981 a six-year-old Italian boy, Alfredo Rampi, fell eighty metres down a narrow well shaft.
For three days rescue teams tried every means they could to bring him out, and the mission was watched around the world on television.
He was dead by the time he was brought to the surface.
At the same time space probes were landing on, and returning safely from, the moon.

SHAFTS OF DARKNESS

All the wisdom of civilisation, all the experts of society,
and the elected leaders of nations
conspire to assail us with a daily barrage
of carnage and bloodshed, guerrilla war and civil strife.

We used to listen with interest to news of the world:
Sport and The Arts were only the cream on the top;
but now the berry is mildewed and dank -
even the avid newsreader no longer tells the time
from bulletin to bulletin.

Foreign lands that lure us in glowing terms of glossy pages
to their brand of domestic crisis can keep it to themselves.
The mass has rejected the media, for its message.

The bomb explodes.   The king is killed.
The anarchist walks free without demur.

It takes an earth-shattering, mind-breaking,
soul-destroying scene of indescribable dimensions
to pull us all together -
of seventy-two hours, Italian fields,
an uncomprehending mother,
and six only years of life -
beyond the world's resources
in shafts of darkness more distant than the moon.

'Awakening', Strangford Lough, County Down

AWAKENING

When we were young
our lives were measured by here and now.
Nothing was that could not be seen, heard, felt.
The sea was for swimming and trees were for climbing.
We ate and we played, and we slept.

As we grew older
our lives became sufficient for our living.
The horizon stretched further, and awareness was deeper.
We started to love the sea and the trees for themselves.
We learned and we loved, but still we slept.

Was the growth of awareness
a loss of innocence or an awakening?
- when the uncomplicated love of our childhood
became the courtship of minds and bodies,
stirring the seed-pods of sexuality.

And the emotional recesses of the mind left
the sea crashing in our ears
long after we had left the shore,
the trees weaving an eternal backcloth
for our thoughts.

After the awakening
we now settle uneasily to wait for each new spring,
uncertain of its source or destination.
Is it a surging sea that comes to drown our human senses?
- a falling tree to crush our mortal hopes?

Is it the last awakening of our life - our death?

METAMORPHOSIS

The happy traveller
closed his eyes
and found himself
in paradise
another lifetime's
due reward
in chiropteractic
form revived;

Hanging inertly
from the roof
swaying in
subterranean cave
responding to
the earthly thrusts
blindly to each
vibrating wave.

Rejoicing in
another life
he felt
a thrilling hand entwined
and slender fingers
lightly held
as a sleeping
head inclined
to join his
closing eyes in rest
against an arm
and briefly blind.

Turning with a
sideways glance
he saw the
calmly resting form
in all the bustle
as in trance
relaxing chrysalis
in rush-hour flap
an arm upstretched
in gentle shape
to reach the
metro ceiling-strap.

THE ACCOUNT

Anne-Marie was one of the quietest girls.
In class she never volunteered an answer,
and, when spoken to, her replies were brief
and so quiet you could hardly hear her.

When it came to her turn to contribute
to the September ritual of talking
about the 'most memorable day of the holidays'
no-one expected very much.

Nobody was really listening when she began
by saying that it was the sixteenth day of August -
Miss Jones was looking at her watch and thinking
that Anne-Marie wouldn't need the three minutes up to lunch.

"I had spent the day at my gran's,
And she had walked back to our house for her tea."
- by which time whispered conversations
were drowning the main speaker's little tale.

"When I heard the knock on the door
I thought it was my uncle, come to take my granny home.
So I opened the door - and was pushed aside
by two big men with masks and guns."

Miss Jones looked up and wondered how Anne-Marie
could ever conjure up that kind of thing.
And it seemed that someone had waved a magic sword
for all the restless little minds had lost their tongues.

"They made us lie on the floor, and tied our hands.
They stuck some tape across our mouths and eyes.
They said they'd shoot us if we tried to move,
and we shouldn't think of doing something brave.

When Uncle came and knocked the door
they let him come inside and call out for us all.
And then they hit him on the head and took his car,
and said not to move or everyone would be dead.

My granny was the first to free her hands.
She helped us get the tape and biting ropes away.
She told my mum to phone for help,
and wiped my uncle's forehead with a cloth.

In the morning on the news it said the car
had been used in an attack against the police.
Two constables were dead and more were hurt.
'How awful for their families', said my gran."

Ole Bulls plass, Bergen, Norway

THE MUSIC OF LIFE

Nøkken rises from the waters
In Ole Bulls plass.

Children play in the fountain
Their shrieks as sharp as glass.

Sunlight glints on the droplets
Reflecting the sun's weak ray.

Shoppers rush past, laden
With the purchases of the day.

Workers chat in their lunch-time
Enjoying an hour's respite.

Students linger and loiter
Setting the world to right.

An old woman wraps her coat around her,
Cold on any day.

A man with worry on his face
Tries to ease his fears away.

In the background, trade and traffic -
A constant bustle of sound.

But never wavering from their task,
Never diverted by the throng -

Nøkken inspires the great musician,
And Ole Bull lifts the people
With the magic of his silent tune.

Sykkylven, Norway

SYKKYLVEN

If I were free to choose the life
that most appealed to me
I would feel most strongly moved to say
- 'This is the place, this is the time, for me'.

I love the unhindered sense of space;
the land without much detail bound;
the fjord escaping earthly ties;
the air which carries freshness round.

The open landscape seems to say
'This small community is what you see.
Look for no secrets: nothing hides,
no-one intrudes, and everyone is free
- in this quiet place removed from earth's dark corners'.

Of course I know that life is never so
while human inhumanity prevails.
But nonetheless I would persist
hoping this paradise really does exist.

LOOK BRAVELY TO THE FUTURE

I

For nearly two millenia Horace won the war.
Mothers sent their tender babes
And fathers proudly waved good-bye
As striplings donned accoutrements of war
And stepped into the battlefield
With honour so to die.

Dulce et decorum est
pro patria mori.
[Horace]

The twentieth century changed all that,
As Owen and Sassoon laid bare
The harsh realities of fear,
In fields of mud, disease and death
With graphic scenes of limbs asunder
Thrown around the sphere.

My subject is war
and the pity of war.
The Poetry is in the Pity.
[Wilfred Owen]

And for the new millenium
There is the harvest from the strife:
The ploughshares forging from the swords,
The bombs exploding into love,
The armies marching on for peace,
The only weapons words.

They shall beat their swords
into ploughshares and their
spears into pruning hooks;
nation shall not lift up
sword against nation, neither
shall they learn war any more.
[Isaiah 2:4]

LOOK BRAVELY TO THE FUTURE

II

For more than two millenia Judaic hatred raged:
proclaiming single deity,
preserving racial purity,
parading proud inheritance of choice -
a kosher cocktail; an almost
exterminating trinity.

Keeping biblical prediction, the chosen race dispersed
(to some extent the consequence
of self-imposed distress);
from early Christian condemnation
through mediaeval persecution
to pogrom, ghetto, holocaustic Shoah –
prolonged and ugly as the words themselves.

Latterly a new and promised land
- a mirage or a vision? -
glimpsed darkly by a yellow star,
as disunited churches point
their self-accusing spires and prostrate lie
before their patriarchal mother creed.

A TIME OF TRUTH
(for Sandy 1946-1998)

They told us it would be difficult,
to cope with inevitable death -
that the signs would be misleading,
we would have unsustainable faith.

They told us it would be hard
to accept what the surgeons would say;
that outward appearances would lead us
to think in a miracle's way.

They told us it wouldn't be easy
(when all the evidence conveyed
that clutching at straws was the answer)
to face reality instead.

The lies we believed to be true
we fed like a drip every day:
talk of tomorrow, next week, and next month -
there was always something to say.

The pain we tried to keep hidden
(and wondered if she hid it too)
was a mutual bond of unspeaking
in conversations truly untrue.

The love beyond explanation
took us down to the regions of death.
One breathing without comprehension,
others fighting emotion for breath.

How difficult, how hard was it all?
How well did we cope with the blow?

Certain things can not be translated.
You do not know until you know.

Åsane Church, Bergen, Norway

THE CHURCH AT ÅSANE, Norway

Here are no dark satanic walls,
No bogeymen from childhood days,
No devil's tunes to twist my mind,
No clammy hands to force my ways.

The church which brightly confronts me
Basking in pale winter sunlight
Reflects the heaven's rays.

The music that richly surrounds me
Plays unfamiliar melodies
In familiar harmony.

The people who warmly embrace me
Can read the turmoil of my mind
And melt my frozen tears.

The arms that gently enfold me
And guide me to the Bread of Life
Make manifest His love:

The love that strongly assures me
In fellowship and prayers
Reaches my darkest hours.

All these clear signs - and much, much more -
Are the living God who loves me
And says to his unworthy servant,
'Be strong in faith. Go forth in peace'.

FROM A MIDNIGHT SUN

Then, in my saddest year,
you brought bright glimpses from a midnight sun.

Now, to lonely moments,
you bring rich memories of laughter.

These things endure,
transforming the raindrops of sorrow on my glasses
into the rainbow colours of happiness and joy.

In times of sadness or sorrow think on that moment -
and know that it is good to have such friends.

'Looking down on azure seas', Northern Ireland

TOMORROW
(for Orsi)

No feelings of guilt,
no agonised thoughts,
just a crystal-clear message
promising

- elevated thoughts,
high hopes,
exciting ideas,
exhilarating fantasies;

- inspiring dreams
soaring beyond reality,
new life in notions
and hope on fire;

daytime adventures
and night-time imaginings;
- lying on a grassy slope,
beneath a clear blue sky,
looking down on azure seas,
caressing a heart's desire.

'A myriad of leaf and flower', Fayrer House, Lake District, England

CASCADE OF MEMORIES

Around a corner of my life
I saw a princess from afar
enwreathed in sweetly scented air –
a myriad of leaf and flower.

And all the atmosphere was charged with love,
as nature meant our lives to be:
removed from troubles, care and woe –
indulged in magic luxury.

Cares may return and pleasures dim
but we will never lose those realms
as quiet notes of life's sweet tunes
permeate from distant dreams.

INCUBUS

A mesmerising spell -
fearful, deadly, stark -
a convoluted image
intense and sharp and dark -
disrupts the peaceful sleeping mind
with flashes hot that spark
a frantic scene of fantasy
of hectic noise and din.
With chilling force and numbing awe
a serpent breaks the skin
and slow emerges from the breast
corrupting from within.

Then all the loving guardian forces
in universal language sought her.
Combined to save the shattered heart
with swift, decisive, cutting slaughter -
to break the penetrating force
which violates their dearest daughter.

To the Most Rev. P. Remigius, D.D., Bishop of Kumbakonam
- with grateful thanks

THE BISHOP'S INVITATION

with persuasive exhortation
was a quick perambulation
to the holy ground.

The day's road was long and turning,
the earth was light and burning.
It answered mental yearning
to reach the holy ground.

I felt my faith restore
as we walked the corridor
to the welcome open door
of my private holy ground.

Was Saint Peter there to meet me?
Were Archangels there to greet me?
What treasures there would treat me
at the promised holy ground?

The Bishop's final guile
- presented with a smile -
was a grinning crocodile
to guard the holy ground!

City Scenes, Budapest, Hungary

BUDAPEST

From prehistoric early morning mists
To midnight's futuristic lights
Pulsating silent Danube flows
Through history's, city's, people's days and nights.

Descending from surrounding hills and plains
Seven wandering tribes conclude nomadic ways
And in a beaker's blood a contract make -
A Carpathian Plain of Paradise.

Kaleidoscope of princes and palaces
Heroes and horses, castles and kings,
Byzantine, Asiatic, Jewish, Christian and Muslim,
Arpad and Stephen - an awesome confusion of things ….

Two million people piled high, snaked long,
Ten thousand tenemented palaces unfold,
With lines and cables, metros, trams and trains
Interleaved with lives untold.

A seething mass of movement, innumerable individuals,
Anonymous and indistinguishable
Dividing into human elements - then coming to life
Through personal encounter.

'Freezing Mists of Winter Time' — *northern Hungary*

TRAVELLING NORTH

There is no end to the white fog
and freezing mists of winter time
which link the drifting snows and heavy skies
from late November until the middle of March.

Incredible incidents of nature
crack the ghostly shroud of frozen scenes
as a white hare struggles in slow loping movements
across our view, extending a mirage of action
in the eerily silent surroundings.

Storks' nests, abandoned temporarily,
survive the rigours of gale-force winds,
snow-storms and blizzards,
like sentries perched on high,
waiting for the end of bitter purgatory.

The dogs which guard the isolated houses
bark hoarse and feeble signals of our passing,
then muster up the strength to nourish their weak frames
with a few mouthfuls from their bowls of freezing scraps
before retreating to what comfort they can find
against the most sheltered gable wall.

The snowdrops of earlier years are distant memories
of new life which came and went, now lost in forgetfulness,
like lines of sparsely vegetated trees
pointing to dim and hazy paths,
leading uncertainly towards nothingness.

The long slow coldness numbs body, mind and soul,
reflecting nature's rote in human pain.
Patiently we await the end of this unliving
until the world from which we came revives again.

But there is no certainty that it will ever come.
Expectation is absent and hope an alien thought
as in the mind there is no end
to the white fog and freezing mists of winter time.

WHEN TIME HEALS
(for Emily)

If only we could turn back time
and days and nights could disappear:
our lives and loves would know no bounds,
our joys would vanquish every fear.

We cried for you and prayed for you,
as we learnt the details of your plight.
We beg an act of your forgiveness
for which we have no claim nor right.

We only hope our country's shame
strengthens your visionary embrace –
and creates a generous state of mind
whereby your family can show us grace.

When time heals and the hurt passes,
when life presents a fresh perspective:
then have no doubt that all is good
and see experience as new directive.

Now part of you is in my existence,
prompting deeds I must fulfill.
I'll treasure it, and its importance
in life's destiny -
(So I will!)

TROUBLED TIMES
(for Mark 1967-2002)

Before your life was hardly ended
I stood at Menin Gate
And listened to the Last Post sounded
For fallen men of conflicts great.

I have no doubt your fight was just
As great as theirs within your mind;
Your sacrifice to cause unknown,
The grief as great you left behind.

Troubled times bring troubled minds.
We all must share collective guilt –
And we would gladly give our all
To see a lost life new rebuilt.

All we can do who stay behind
Is promise never to betray
The human energy and love
That you engendered every day.

Selja Island, Norway   *The Church at Selje*

According to legend, Sunniva was the daughter of an Irish chieftain and lived in the tenth century. Her father was killed by Viking invaders, whose leader sought to marry her. She rejected his advances and fled by boat with a number of her supporters. Their journey ended on the island of Selja, off the coast of Norway. They sought refuge in a cave, which was then sealed by a landslide.

Many years later the cave was found with the remains of Sunniva, which emitted a sweet perfume. Some visitors claim to see the image of Sunniva in the rocks of the cave.

She became recognised as one of the four saints of Norway, and in 1996 special celebrations were held to commemorate the one thousandth year of her sanctification.

In front of the altar of the present day church in the mainland town of Selje, opposite which the island of Selja is situated, is an Irish processional cross, presented to the church on the occasion of the millennial celebrations in 1996 by members of the church at Åsane, Bergen.

The Celtic design of the cross was strongly influenced by the Viking invasions of Ireland during the 9th and 10th centuries. The shaft of the cross is made from a piece of Irish Bog Oak 3,500 years old.

SELJA AND SUNNIVA

What hand of chance, or destiny, or fate,
ordained a voyage bold across the seas –
to lands unknown, and perilous existence fraught
with dangers foreign, and devoid of faith?

Three boats committed to the winds severe
that drove them round Britannia's wildest coasts
and on to Norway's unforgiving edge -
a harsh and cynical twist of fate, by God!

In virgin flight across the unknown seas
to Viking lands the currents strong did bring
- unkindly forced by Norseman's lustful eyes –
the daughter of a slaughtered Celtic king.

A Christian moment of explosive love
pre-empting late protesting creeds
then left exposed upon an island bare
the seeds of Reformation care.

And in a hillside cave unmarked,
a miracle of preservation:
an image on a rock, that was to spark
millennial fragrance sweetly offering

ecumenic light from dark

Giant's Causeway, Northern Ireland

LIVING THE DAY

There are meetings in life which race by in moments,
Encounters which seem to be gone in a flash,
Conversations for minutes which should last for ever,
Times when eternity just does not last.

And then there are moments which linger too long,
And comments which wrongly portray a bad grace.
Brief witless remarks which destroy good relations,
And flippant responses unworthy of space.

The balancing act between living and life
Might lie in thinking a lateral way,
And differently placing it all in perspective
By losing the darkness and living the day.

THE CYCLE

She chanced upon a broken man
and offered patience, love and energy.
She took the shattered fragments of his heart
and gently placed the pieces back again.

They shared enchantment and idyllic days,
a world of elegance and courtly scenes,
meeting and matching aspirations,
a lady and a gentleman upon a global stage.

Who can account for what befalls?
Or explain in terms of destiny or fate?
Is it humanity in acts of strength
(or weakness) or simply chance that calls?

As lady-like she pirouettes another dance,
natural and native in its origins.
And like a gentleman he slips
discreetly to the dark again.

NOTES

p 7   *A Reminder of Humility* — presented to the poet by a young student as a leaving gift. Gavin Weston is now a well-known local artist.

P 26   *Metamorphosis* — inspired by the observation of exhausted commuters on a crowded underground train during the rush-hour.

p 28   *The Account* — the record of a true incident in a school in Northern Ireland, and representative of the experiences of many children during 'The Troubles'.

p 31   *The Music of Life* — Ole Bull was a celebrated Norwegian musician. Nøkken was a water nymph in Norwegian mythology.

p 47   *Incubus* — an interpretation of a young lady's nightmare at a time when she was involved in an illicit relationship.

p 49   *The Bishop's Invitation* — while staying as a house guest with the Bishop of Kumbakonam in India, the writer was called by the distressed occupant of a neighbouring room, who had discovered a lizard in the lavatory bowl in her bathroom. Their panic at such an everyday event was the source of much amusement during the subsequent dinner party.

p 55   *When Time Heals* - as a young American graduate Emily spent some months researching the conflict in Northern Ireland. During that time she was the victim of a terrifying ordeal at the hands of some sinister forces. Her safe emergence was a source of great relief for all who knew her, and also of shame that her perception of an essentially hospitable community should be tarnished in this way.

p 57   *Troubled Times* - a tribute to Mark, a young husband and father, for whom the pressures of modern living and society were to prove too much. The Menin Gate is a war memorial in Ypres, Belgium, to soldiers who died during the First World War.